BRILLIANT BRITS

SHAKESPEARE

RICHARD BRASSEY

Orion
Children's Books

Who was the most famous writer who ever lived?

Who has had more written about him than any other person who ever lived?

Whose plays are always being performed somewhere in the world?

Who might not even have written the plays he is so famous for?

WILLIAM SHAKESPEARE
or – as he always was known in the theatre – WILL

Will was born in a house which still stands in the small market town of Stratford-upon-Avon. His father John was a glovemaker and his mother, Mary Arden, the daughter of a farmer. Will was the oldest of six (though one of his sisters died when she was only eight).

Even though Will's father became mayor of Stratford, he probably didn't know how to write. This has made some people believe that Will could never have grown up to be the greatest writer of all time.

But Will almost certainly got a good education at the King's School just down the road. All his lessons would have been in Latin. He would have read exciting stories and plays by ancient Roman authors.

The schoolroom can still be seen upstairs in what was then the Town Hall. In the room below, groups of travelling actors often put on plays. We can't be sure, but it seems likely that Will would have seen at least some of them.

THE FOREST OF ARDEN

STRATFORD-UPON-AVON
where Will was born, grew up and retired

MARY ARDEN'S HOUSE
where his mum grew up

ANNE HATHAWAY'S COTTAGE
where his wife grew up

HALL'S CROFT
where his daughter lived

HOLY TRINITY CHURCH
where he's buried

THE GUILDHALL
with the schoolroom upstairs

'The whining schoolboy with his satchel and shining morning face creeping like a snail unwillingly to school'

Perhaps Will was remembering his walk to school when he wrote these lines.

THE BIRTHPLACE
where he grew up

CHARLCOTE PARK
where he is said to have gone deer-poaching

NEW PLACE
The second biggest house in town, which Will must have passed every day on the way to school and which he eventually bought and retired to.

LONDON

CLOPTON BRIDGE

RIVER AVON

So little is known about Will's life from the time he left school until he was 28 that these have been called . . . 'the Lost Years'.

It's quite likely that he worked as a teacher in Lancashire. He may even have toured the country with a group of actors.

A popular legend says he had to run away to London after he was caught poaching deer.

The most fanciful suggestion is that he sailed round the world with Sir Francis Drake and was shipwrecked. This is almost certainly nonsense – though he did write about being shipwrecked in one of his last plays, *The Tempest*.

The only thing we know for sure is that in 1582, when he was 18, he married a farmer's daughter named Anne Hathaway. Next year they had a daughter, Susanna, and two years after that, twins called Hamnet and Judith. They probably all moved in with Will's parents, but at some point Will left for London alone.

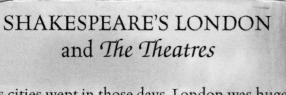

SHAKESPEARE'S LONDON
and *The Theatres*

As cities went in those days, London was huge
... ten times bigger than any other town in
England. Will seems to have joined an acting
group at a theatre called ... the Theater!
The law said all theatres had to be built
outside the walls of the City, or on
the south bank of the Thames.

ST PAUL'S
CATHEDRAL

*The Fortune
Theatre*

WHITEHALL PALACE
where the Queen lived

BLACKFRIARS
GATEHOUSE
where Will lived in 1613

The Swan Theatre

RIVER THAMES

The Bear Garden

*The Rose
Theatre*

*The Globe
Theatre*

The south bank was where bear-baiting, bullfighting, cockfighting, juggling and all sorts of other entertainment went on.

The Theater

The Curtain Theatre

SILVER STREET
where Will lived in 1604

CRIPPLEGATE

BISHOP'S GATE

THE TOWER
OF LONDON

LONDON WALL

ST MARY
OVERY
now called
Southwark
Cathedral

LONDON BRIDGE
with chopped-off
heads on stakes

Will must have been in London for some time by 1592 when we first hear of one of his plays being performed at a south bank theatre called the Rose. He had also, apparently, become quite well-known as an actor.

An actor's life was very hard. Will's company would have put on a different play every day except Sunday. Actors had to learn hundreds of parts in a year. Yet somehow Will found time to write plays. By 1592 he had written at least four, and other writers were starting to get jealous of his success.

In Will's time lots of people thought the theatre was fantastic, but others, known as Puritans, thought it was an evil place where lazy people went to avoid work. They also believed that the crowds caused the plague. When plague broke out the theatres had to shut.

Will's plays were only gathered together and printed seven years after his death. He evidently wrote very fast, but nothing we know of survives in his handwriting except some signatures, all of which look different. We don't even know how he spelt his name!

Will is believed to have written thirty-seven plays during his twenty-five-odd years in London. He probably wrote quite a few more which have been lost.

Will pinched stories from all over the place. He seldom made up his own. But this doesn't mean he was a bad writer. He transformed these stories into magical plays full of amazing characters and situations.

Will's life seems boring compared to some other playwrights of the time. Ben Jonson killed an actor in a duel. Christopher Marlowe was stabbed to death and may have been a spy. But everybody agreed that Will was the best at writing plays. He also wrote many poems called sonnets. The sonnets are full of mysteries that people still argue about.

Will probably only visited his family once a year. By 1597 he had made enough money to move them into the second largest house in Stratford. He must have been sad at the time, for his son Hamnet had just died, aged eleven.

Will wrote all sorts of plays – funny ones, plays about historical characters, and exciting romantic ones. There's something for everybody. But they can be difficult to understand. English was rather different when Will was writing 400 years ago. It helps to know the story before seeing the plays.

A good play to start with is A *Midsummer Night's Dream*, because it's funny. A group of people get in a muddle in a wood when the fairies put spells on them. Even the Queen of the Fairies is under a spell so when she wakes up she falls in love with the first person she sees ... a poor man called Bottom who's been given the head of a donkey by another fairy. Confused? You can see why it helps to know what's going on!

'What angel wakes me from my flowery bed?'

'Oh Romeo, Romeo,
Wherefore art thou Romeo?'

Another very popular play is *Romeo and Juliet*. This is much more like real life. Romeo and Juliet fall in love but their families hate each other. Secretly they marry, but the family feud eventually leads to disaster.

In the famous balcony scene Romeo talks to Juliet from beneath her bedroom window.

'It is my love!'

In 1598 the Puritan who owned the land where the Theater stood demanded a lot more rent. On a snowy winter's night Will's group of actors secretly took it to bits, carried it across London Bridge and put it back together on the south bank. They renamed it the Globe.

Will was a part owner of the Globe until it burnt down after a cannon was fired on stage during one of his last plays. The only casualty was a groundling whose breeches caught fire. Fortunately he managed to douse the flames with his bottle of beer. Otherwise he would surely have burned to death.

Groundlings paid one penny to stand in front of the stage. They drank beer, ate nuts and shouted at the actors. It cost more to sit in the galleries. If you were very posh, you could hire a stool and sit on the stage, smoking your pipe.

A few years ago a new Globe was built near the site to look as much like the old Globe as possible. You can see Will's plays performed there every summer.

Most people think Will's best plays are the four great tragedies which were first performed at the Globe. A tragedy is a play where the main character makes mistakes which lead to an unhappy ending.

Hamlet

This is Will's most famous play. Hamlet's father's ghost tells Hamlet he's been murdered. Hamlet makes everything worse by not being able to decide what to do about it. In one famous scene he discusses his problems with a skull.

Macbeth

Macbeth is told by three witches that he will become King of Scotland. Egged on by his scheming wife, he kills the king and steals the throne. But the old king's son brings an army to avenge his father, and Macbeth is doomed.

Othello

Othello, the black general of
the Venetian army, has just
married beautiful Desdemona.
But his lieutenant Iago has a
secret grudge against him and
can't bear to see him happy.
He tells Othello that
Desdemona is cheating on him.
In a rage Othello smothers her.
Then he discovers that she was
innocent all along.

'Blow, winds, and
crack your cheeks!
Rage! Blow!'

'I loved not wisely
but too well.'

King Lear

Old King Lear divides his
kingdom between two of his
daughters but gives nothing to
Cordelia, the youngest, because
she refuses to flatter him.
The other two soon throw
Lear out of his own castle.
He wanders alone on a stormy
heath at night. Cordelia
comes to the rescue, but this
is a tragedy so it has to
end badly . . .

Queen Elizabeth I had often enjoyed Will's plays, which were put on specially for her at the palace. James I, who succeeded her, found plays rather boring, but his wife and son were crazy about them. Will's company became known as the King's Men, and his plays were performed at court constantly.

THE EARL OF OXFORD

CARDINAL WOLSEY

CHRISTOPHER MARLOWE

FRANCIS BACON

There are many mysteries connected with the plays, and many scholars have spent a lifetime trying to prove that Will couldn't possibly have written them. Here are some of the people they think might have written them instead. It's even been suggested that Queen Elizabeth wrote the plays, though how she continued to do so after her death is not explained.

Even if you believe Will did not write the plays . . . you owe a lot to whoever did. When Dr Johnson wrote the first real English dictionary 150 years later he took more examples of how to use words from Will than from any other writer.

All sorts of expressions that we use today without thinking come directly from the plays.

Just as Will pinched most of the stories for his plays, many writers since have taken Will's plays and characters and turned them into films, musicals, books and even plays of their own.

There has hardly been a day in the last 400 years when one or more of Will's plays was not being performed somewhere in the world ... in a theatre, in a park, on a ship, in a school, on the radio, on TV, in a film. They can equally well be produced on a stage with elaborate sets and costumes or in a bare room with everyday clothes.

Will is the most famous writer who ever lived. Yet he left very little behind, apart from his writing, and much of what he did has disappeared.

His chair survived for a century or two but so many bits were cut off it by souvenir hunters that now there's nothing left.

A crabapple tree he was said to have slept under suffered the same fate.

Is this a leaking tap which I see before me?

Well met, good dog

In Victorian times there lived a spotted dog which was confidently said to have been descended from Shakespeare's own hound.

Even the birthplace nearly got taken to America by P T Barnum, the circus owner.

Will had only one grandchild and she died without any children. His sister Joan married a hatter called William Hart. They had a great-grandson called Shakespeare Hart, who was a plumber. Joan's descendants are the only people who can claim any sort of connection with Will today.

At the age of 52 Shakespeare fell ill and died. He had given up writing plays and was living back in Stratford, where apparently friends such as Ben Jonson visited him. He may have taken up gardening. We know that he put on weight. Oddly, in his will he left his second-best bed to his wife – though why only the second best, and who got the best, is unclear!

A few years after his death a monument was erected in Stratford, in Holy Trinity Church. It has a bust which people who knew Shakespeare said looked like him. Perhaps he knew how famous he would become, for on his grave are the words: 'Curst be he that moves my bones.' So far as we know, no one has.